THE LORD IS MY
SHEPHERD

Copyright © 1982 Lion Publishing

Published by
Lion Publishing plc
Sandy Lane West, Littlemore, Oxford, England
ISBN 0 85648 364 8 (casebound edition)
ISBN 0 7459 1071 8 (paperback edition)
Albatross Books Pty Ltd
PO Box 320, Sutherland, NSW 2232, Australia
ISBN 0 86760 365 8 (casebound edition)
ISBN 0 86760 692 4 (paperback edition)

Compiled by Ruth Connell

First edition 1982
Reprinted 1983, 1986
First paperback edition 1986
Reprinted 1988, 1989

Psalm 23 quoted from *The Holy Bible,
New International Version:* copyright © New York
International Bible Society, 1978

Other Bible quotations from:
Authorized King James Version of the Bible,
Crown copyright.
Revised Standard Version, copyright 1946 and
1952, second edition 1971, Division of Christian
Education, National Council of the Churches of
Christ in the USA

British Library Cataloguing in Publication Data
[Bible. O.T. Psalms XXIII. *English. New
International. 1985]*
The Lord is my shepherd - (Famous Bible passages)
I. The Lord is my shepherd II. Connell, Ruth
III. Series
223/.205206 BS1424
ISBN 0 85648 364 8

Printed and bound in Hong Kong

Famous Bible Passages

THE LORD IS MY SHEPHERD

Psalm 23

A LION BOOK

Oxford · Batavia · Sydney

The Lord is my shepherd, I shall lack nothing.
He makes me lie down in green pastures,
he leads me beside quiet waters,
he restores my soul.
He guides me in paths of righteousness
for his name's sake.
Even though I walk through the valley of the shadow of death,
I will fear no evil,
for you are with me;
your rod and your staff,
they comfort me.
You prepare a table before me
in the presence of my enemies.
You anoint my head with oil;
my cup overflows.
Surely goodness and love will follow me
all the days of my life,
and I will dwell in the house of the Lord
for ever.

Psalm 23

The Lord is my shepherd

The Sovereign Lord . . . tends his flock like a shepherd:
He gathers the lambs in his arms
and carries them close to his heart;
he gently leads those that have young.

Isaiah 40:11

The sweet word 'shepherd' . . . brings to the godly, when they
read it or hear it, as it were a confidence, a consolation, or
security like the word 'father'.

Martin Luther

'The Lord is my shepherd'; if he be a shepherd to no one else,
he is a shepherd to me; he cares for me, watches over me, and
preserves me.

Charles Haddon Spurgeon

Jesus said: 'I am the good shepherd; I know my own and my
own know me, as the Father knows me and I know the
Father; and I lay down my life for the sheep.'

John 10:14–15

I shall lack nothing

Glory in God who provides all, and above all, desires to impart himself.

Thomas à Kempis

The Lord first — the Lord as the Owner, the Ruler, the Provider, the Guide — and all fear of want and all fear of failure are gone.

Hudson Taylor

God is ever giving to his children, yet hath not the less. His riches are imparted, not impaired.

Thomas Watson

All the good things you love come from God, but they are pleasant and good only as they relate to him.

St Augustine

I might want otherwise, but when the Lord is my Shepherd he is able to supply my needs, and he is certainly willing to do so, for his heart is full of love, and therefore 'I shall not want.' I shall not lack for temporal things. Does he not feed the ravens, and cause the lilies to grow? How, then, can he leave his children to starve? I shall not want for spirituals, I know that his grace will be sufficient for me. Resting in him he will say to me, 'As thy days so shall thy strength be.' I may not possess all that I wish for, but 'I shall not want.'

Charles Haddon Spurgeon

The man who has God for his treasure has all things in One. Many ordinary treasures may be denied him, or if he is allowed to have them, the enjoyment of them will be so tempered that they will never be necessary to his happiness. Or if he must see them go, one after one, he will scarcely feel a sense of loss, for having the Source of all things he has in One all satisfaction, all pleasure, all delight.

A. W. Tozer

My God will meet all your needs according to his glorious riches in Christ Jesus.

Philippians 4:19

*H*e makes me lie down in green pastures

Thou hast formed us for thyself, and our hearts are restless till they find rest in thee.
St Augustine

The rest he offers is the rest of meekness, the blessed relief which comes when we accept ourselves for what we are and cease to pretend.
A. W. Tozer

Jesus I come to rest in the knowledge that you are all I need.
Ulrich Schaffer

In peace I will both lie down and sleep;
for thou alone, O Lord, makest me dwell in safety.
Psalm 4:8

*H*e leads me beside quiet waters

The proud and covetous are never at rest, but the poor and
humble in spirit pass their lives in an abundance of peace.
Thomas à Kempis

'Be still, and know that I am God.'
Psalm 46:10

By pastures green he leads me,
With gladness there he feeds me,
From purest springs revives me,
In need he counsel gives me.
Paul Gerhardt

Jesus said, 'Every one who drinks of this water will thirst
again, but whoever drinks of the water that I shall give him
will never thirst; the water that I shall give him will become
in him a spring of water welling up to eternal life.'
John 4:13–14

*H*e restores my soul

This is what the Sovereign Lord says: I myself will search for my sheep and look after them. As a shepherd looks after his scattered flock when he is with them, so will I look after them. I will rescue them from all the places where they were scattered on a day of clouds and darkness.

Ezekiel 34:11–12

The retrieving or reviving of the sheep pictures the deeper renewal of the man of God, spiritually perverse or ailing as he may be.

Derek Kidner

The same hand which first rescued us from ruin, reclaims us from all our subsequent aberrations.

J. Thornton

When the soul grows sorrowful he revives it; when it is sinful he sanctifies it; when it is weak he strengthens it.

Charles Haddon Spurgeon

It is God the eternal, the immeasurable, the filler of all things, who alone can solace the soul and bring true joy to the heart.

Thomas à Kempis

*Those who hope in the Lord
will renew their strength.
They will soar on wings like eagles;
they will run and not grow weary,
they will walk and not be faint.*

Isaiah 40:31

*H*e guides me in paths of righteousness

God who made thee for thy life, and thy life for thee, can direct thee, and he only.

F. B. Meyer

Trust in the Lord with all thine heart; and lean not unto thine own understanding. In all thy ways acknowledge him, and he shall direct thy paths.

Proverbs 3 : 5–6

In general . . . the Lord guides and directs his people by affording them, in answer to prayer, the light of his Holy Spirit which enables them to understand and to love the Scriptures. The word of God . . . is to furnish us with just principles, right apprehensions, to regulate our judgements and affections, and thereby to influence and direct our conduct.

John Newton

We come closest to God not when, with our mind, we obtain a wide conspectus of truth, but when in our purposes we are united with his righteous purpose.

William Temple

God has plans — not problems — for our lives . . . The life of a Christian is an education for higher service. No athlete complains when the training is hard. He thinks of the game, or the race.

Corrie ten Boom

I don't believe in coincidence any more
because I know
that that which seems coincidental
is exactly the plan
God is pursuing for my life
with loving certainty.
Ulrich Schaffer

For his name's sake

The name of God is God himself; the nature of God, so far as it can be discovered to man. It means therefore, together with his existence, all his attributes or perfection.
John Wesley

It is not for any good we deserve, or have done, or can do, for which he taketh such care of his weak and foolish children. It is for the glory of his free grace, constant love, and sworn covenant, even for his own name's sake.
David Dickson

The name of the Lord is a strong tower;
the righteous man runs into it and is safe.
Proverbs 18:10

Even though I walk through the valley of the shadow of death

Let him who walks in the dark,
who has no light,
trust in the name of the Lord
and rely on his God.

Isaiah 50:10

When Jesus spoke again to the people, he said, 'I am the light of the world. Whoever follows me will never walk in darkness, but will have the light of life.'

John 8:12

The valley of the shadow of death holds no darkness for the child of God. There must be light, else there could be no shadow. Jesus is the Light. He has overcome death.

Dwight Moody

God . . . often produces the greatest good from those events we are apt to look upon as evil.

John Newton

The suffering and agonizing moments through which I have passed over the last few years have drawn me closer to God.

Martin Luther King Jnr

It is in the valley of the shadow of death that solid, divine comforts are brought to light. But this is not all. The conflict terminates, the darkness passes away; but the spoils are permanent, and the gains are eternal.

Hudson Taylor

I will fear no evil

The Lord watches over you —
the Lord is your shade at your right hand;
the sun will not harm you by day,
nor the moon by night.
The Lord will keep you from all harm —
he will watch over your life.
Psalm 121:5—7

The evil one . . . works with mighty power in the children of
disobedience. But all those who are the children of God by
faith are delivered out of his hands. He may fight against
them; and so he will. But he cannot conquer, unless they betray
their own souls. He may torment for a time, but he cannot
destroy; for God is on their side, who will not fail, in the end,
to 'avenge his own elect, that cry unto him day and night'.
John Wesley

God can bring good from evil, and without God we bring evil
out of good.
Blaise Pascal

---

*F*or you are with me

In the Holy Land . . . the shepherd spends his life with the sheep. He is with them from their birth onwards, day and night, for even when they are driven into a cave or a sheepfold for the night, he never leaves them.

H. V. Morton

Jesus replied, 'If anyone loves me, he will obey my teaching. My Father will love him, and we will come to him and make our home with him.'

John 14:23

I am convinced that neither death nor life, neither angels nor demons, neither the present nor the future, nor any powers, neither height nor depth, nor anything else in all creation, will be able to separate us from the love of God that is in Christ Jesus our Lord.

Romans 8:38–39

Where can I go from your Spirit?
Where can I flee from your presence?
If I go up to the heavens, you are there;
if I make my bed in the depths, you are there.
If I rise on the wings of the dawn,
if I settle on the far side of the sea,
even there your hand will guide me,
your right hand will hold me fast.

Psalm 139:7–9

Your rod and your staff they comfort me

'Because he loves me,' says the Lord, 'I will rescue him;
I will protect him, for he acknowledges my name.
He will call upon me, and I will answer him;
I will be with him in trouble,
I will deliver him and honour him.'

Psalm 91:14–15

'Thy rod and thy staff,' by which thou governest and rulest
thy flock, the ensigns of thy sovereignty and of thy gracious
care.

Charles Haddon Spurgeon

Thy rod chasteneth me when I go astray, and thy staff stayeth
me when I should fall — two things most necessary for me,
good Lord; the one to call me from my fault and error, and
the other to keep me in thy truth and verity.

John Hooper

The staff is essentially a symbol of the concern, the compassion
that a shepherd has for his charges. No other single word can
better describe its function on behalf of the flock than that it is
for their comfort. Whereas the rod conveys the concept of
authority, of power, of discipline, of defence against danger, the
word 'staff' speaks of all that is longsuffering and kind.

Phillip Keller

But oh, how did my soul, at this time, prize the preservation that God did set about his people! Ah, how safely did I see them walk, whom God had hedged in! They were within his care, protection, and special providence; though they were full as bad as I by nature; yet because he loved them, he would not suffer them to fall without the range of mercy.

John Bunyan

True believers, although they dwell safely under the protection of God, are, notwithstanding, exposed to many dangers, or rather they are liable to all the afflictions which befall mankind in common, that they may the better feel how much they need the protection of God.

John Calvin

You prepare a table before me

The Lord . . . has filled the hungry with good things.
Luke 1:53

Because your love is better than life,
my lips will glorify you.
I will praise you as long as I live,
and in your name I will lift up my hands.
My soul will be satisfied as with the richest of foods;
with singing lips my mouth will praise you.
Psalm 63:3–5

God provides for his people, not only food and rest, but
refreshment also and pleasure.
Matthew Henry

The prospect is better than a feast. In the Old Testament
world, to eat and drink at someone's table created a bond of
mutual loyalty, and could be the culminating token of a
covenant . . . So to be God's guest is to be more than an
acquaintance, invited for a day. It is to live with him.
Derek Kidner

In the presence of my enemies

We are more than conquerors through him who loved us.
Romans 8:37

We are not delivered out of the world, but, being born from above, we have victory over it. And we have that victory in the same sense, and with the same unfailing certainty, that light overcame darkness.
Watchman Nee

A man with God is always in the majority.
John Knox

You anoint my head with oil

You love righteousness and hate wickedness;
therefore God, your God,
has set you above your companions
by anointing you with the oil of joy.

Psalm 45:7

Lord, thou dost so anoint and make glad our minds with
thine Holy Spirit, that no adversities nor troubles can make us
sorry.

John Hooper

It is God who makes both us and you stand firm in Christ.
He anointed us, set his seal of ownership on us, and put his
Spirit in our hearts as a deposit, guaranteeing what is to come.

1 Corinthians 1:21—22

My cup overflows

Happiness is neither without nor within us.
It is in God, both without and within us.
Blaise Pascal

Paul made a great and noble statement to the Philippians. To those who, in material things, were almost his sole supporters he dared to say, 'I have all things and abound.' Paul gave no hint of need, but took the position of a wealthy child of a wealthy Father, and he had no fears that by so doing he might discourage further supplies . . .

It dishonours the Lord when a representative of his discloses needs that would provoke pity on the part of his hearers. If we have a living faith in God, we shall always make our boast in him.

Watchman Nee

Jesus said: 'I have come that they may have life, and have it to the full.'
John 10:10

Surely goodness . . . will follow me all the days of my life

What exalts God most completely in our mind is not that he is so great or that he is so powerful, but that he is so good.

William Temple

Goodness supplies our needs, and mercy blots out our sins.

Charles Haddon Spurgeon

If God's goodness to us be like the morning light, which shines more and more to the perfect day, let not ours to him be like the morning cloud and the early dew that passeth away.

Matthew Henry

*S*urely . . . *love will follow me all the days of my life*

Surely goodness and mercy shall follow me all the days of my life . . .

King James Version

The steadfast love of the Lord never ceases,
his mercies never come to an end;
they are new every morning;
great is his faithfulness.

Lamentations 3:22–23

It makes a vast difference whether we suppose that God loves us because we are lovable, or that he loves, in spite of much in us which deserves his antagonism, because he is overflowing love.

William Temple

I never saw those heights and depths in grace, and love, and mercy, as I saw after this temptation. Great sins do draw out great grace; and where guilt is most terrible and fierce there the mercy of God in Christ, when showed to the soul, appears most high and mighty.

John Bunyan

The God of Abraham, the God of Isaac, the God of Jacob,
the God of the Christians, is a God of love and consolation;
he is a God who fills the heart and soul of those whom he
possesses; he is a God who makes them feel a profound sense of
their wretchedness and of his infinite mercy; who unites himself
with their inmost soul; who fills it with humility, joy,
confidence and love; who renders them incapable of any end
other than Himself.

Blaise Pascal

And I will dwell in the house of the Lord for ever.

Made as we were in the image of God we scarcely find it strange to take again our God as our All. God was the original habitat and our hearts cannot but feel at home when they enter again that ancient and beautiful abode.

A. W. Tozer

A man's greatest care should be for that place where he lives longest; therefore eternity should be his scope.

Thomas Manton

Dwelling in the house of Jehovah does not mean frequenting his sanctuary, but being a member of his household and an inmate of his family, enjoying his protection, holding communion with him, and subsisting on his bounty.

J. A. Alexander

All who are led by the Spirit of God are sons of God . . . When we cry, 'Abba! Father!' it is the Spirit himself bearing witness with our spirit that we are children of God, and if children, then heirs, heirs of God and fellow heirs with Christ.

Romans 8:14—17

Jesus said: 'Let not your hearts be troubled; believe in God,
believe also in me. In my Father's house are many rooms; if it
were not so, would I have told you that I go to prepare a place
for you? And when I go and prepare a place for you, I will
come again and will take you to myself, that where I am you
may be also.'
John 14:1-3

From thee, great God, we spring, to thee we tend —
Path, motive, guide, original and end.
Boethius

Prayer

*Dear Lord and God! O Holy One, O Lover of my soul!
when you come to my heart, all that is within me will leap up
for joy. You are my glory, the rejoicing of my heart. You are
my hope and my refuge in my hour of peril.*

*Yet I am still weak in love, imperfect in goodness, and I need
your strength and comfort. So visit me often and teach me by
your holy discipline; free me from evil passions, and cure my
heart of all its undisciplined emotions; then I shall be healthy
and clean within, made fit for loving, strong for suffering,
steadfast for enduring.*

Thomas à Kempis

Quotations from copyright material are as follows:
St Augustine, The Confessions of Augustine in
Modern English, *translated by Sherwood Eliot Wirt,*
Zondervan Publishers 1971, Lion Publishing 1978;
Corrie ten Boom, Tramp for the Lord, *Hodder and*
Stoughton and Christian Literature Crusade 1974;
Phillip Keller, A Shepherd looks at Psalm 23,
Zondervan Publishing House 1970, Pickering and
Inglis 1976; Thomas à Kempis, The Imitation of
Christ, *translated by Betty I. Knott, Collins Fontana*
1963; Derek Kidner, Psalms 1-72, *Inter-Varsity*
Press 1973; H. V. Morton, In the Steps of the
Master, *Rich and Cowan 1934; Watchman Nee,*
quote page 32 Love not the World, *Victory Press*
1970, quote page 36 A Table in the Wilderness,
Victory Press 1969; Blaise Pascal, Pensées,
translated by John Warrington, J. M. Dent and Sons
1960; Ulrich Schaffer, Greater Than Our Hearts,
Harper and Row 1981; William Temple, in Daily
Readings from William Temple, *compiled by Hugh*
C. Warner, Hodder and Stoughton 1948; A. W.
Tozer, The Pursuit of God, *Christian Publications*
1948, Marshall, Morgan and Scott 1961

Photographs by Colour Library International: page
35; Sister Daniel: pages 17, 26, 30, 43; Fritz
Fankhauser: page 24; Sonia Halliday Photographs:
F. H. C. Birch, page 14, Barry Searle, page 23; Lion
Publishing: David Alexander, pages 11, 13, 18, 21,
29, 41, Jon Willcocks, pages 33, 39; Middle East
Photographic Archive: page 9 and cover; Malcolm
Robertson: page 36